BIRDS *of a* FEATHER
SHOP TOGETHER

BIRDS *of a* FEATHER SHOP TOGETHER

Aesop's Fables for the Fashionable Set

Sandra Bark

Illustrations by Bil Donovan

HARPER DESIGN
An Imprint of HarperCollins Publishers

BIRDS OF A FEATHER SHOP TOGETHER
Aesop's Fables for the Fashionable Set

HarperCollins books may be purchased for
educational, business, or sales promotional use.
For information please write: Special Markets
Department, HarperCollins*Publishers*, 10 East 53rd
Street, New York, NY 10022.

Book design by Iris Shih

First published in 2012 by
Harper Design
An Imprint of HarperCollins*Publishers*
10 East 53rd Street
New York, NY 10022
Tel: (212) 207-7000
Fax: (212) 207-7654
harperdesign@harpercollins.com

Distributed throughout the world by
HarperCollins*Publishers*
10 East 53rd Street
New York, NY 10022
Fax: (212) 207-7654

Library of Congress Number: 2011927593
ISBN 978-0-06-207173-6

Printed in China
First Printing, 2012

For my mother, Brenda, dispenser of morals
and owner of the first pair of heels I ever tried on

CONTENTS

LADIES
WHO
LUNCH

Greta never worked a day in her life. She had a trust fund set up for her by her grandfather—she didn't know how much was in it *exactly*, there were other people who took care of that—and her life was an ongoing series of openings, signings, parties, receptions, dinners, and trips to Tiffany and the couture shows in Paris.

She was having a cocktail at an outdoor café before going on a little shopping spree for a new bauble or two, when her old school friend Anne passed by, lugging a worn leather briefcase.

"Darling, it's been too long!" cried Greta, waving Anne down with her Versace sunglasses. "Stop and have a chat!"

"I can't," said Anne. "I have a meeting."

"That's easy to take care of!" said Greta. "Just call and cancel!"

"I'd love to, believe me," said Anne. "But I just got promoted."

"Oh, my dear Anne!" said Greta, twisting a flawless, pear-shaped, fifty-carat diamond ring around on her finger, "Clearly, you work *too* hard! Sit down and relax. We'll do some shopping, get our nails done, have some fun."

"Sorry, but this girl has to work," said Anne. "Plus, you know, the mortgage is due, credit-card payments are due—blah, blah, blah." She shrugged. "I know it must seem awfully boring to you, but I actually want to retire one day."

"Retire today, darling," suggested Greta. Anne just shook her head and went on her way.

⌁

Forty years later, Greta was living in Miami Beach in a tiny, barely furnished apartment with a tendency to allure vermin. One day, as she was on her way to the grocery store, clad in the latest Salvation Army and counting her food stamps, she caught sight of Anne eating outdoors at the city's poshest restaurant with a group of women. Even from the street Greta could see the table with its plates of steaming lobster and bottles of fine wine, the carefree smiles, and the perfectly manicured fingers. Then she understood:

IT IS BEST TO PREPARE
FOR THE DAYS OF NECESSITY.

ROSALIND
AND THE
BEAUTICIANS

Rosalind had a gift certificate for a facial at a local salon. She almost laughed as she perused the extensive list of treatments promising euphoria, but she made an appointment anyway.

First, she did not like the facial she had booked with the salon's owner, Magda.

"I hate chocolate," she said.

"But you asked for the Cacão Facial," said Magda, "which, if I may say, was emphatically described in our salon brochure as being 'especially for chocolate lovers.'"

"I'd like to try a different service," she said.

Magda shrugged and sent her to Elena.

After Elena had smeared her with cucumber oil and wrapped her in a rosemary-scented bed sheet, Rosalind asked to speak to Magda again.

"I'd like to try a different service," she said. "I smell like a salad."

"That's why it's called a Cucumber and Herb Wrap," explained Magda, who shrugged and sent her to Anya.

Anya scrubbed her with lavender-infused sugar and organic honey, but Rosalind complained.

"Then why did you ask for the Lavender Candy Scrub?" said Magda.

"I'd like to try a different service," said Rosalind. "I hate sweets."

So Magda sent Rosalind to Katrina, even though she was planning to fire Katrina that afternoon because her facials very often resulted in an angry smattering of acne, particularly above the lip and along the jawline.

"Why not?" Magda said to the other girls. "She'll never be happy anyway."

SHE THAT FINDS DISCONTENTMENT IN ONE PLACE IS NOT LIKELY TO FIND HAPPINESS IN ANOTHER.

She perused the extensive list

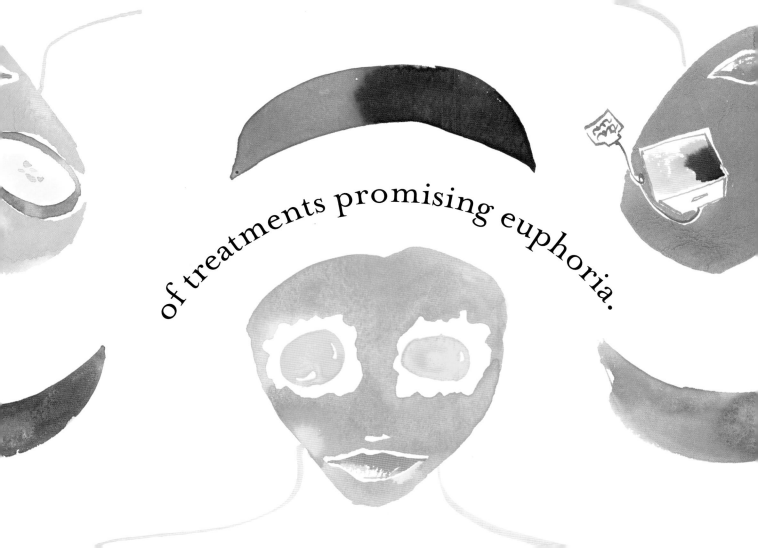

of treatments promising euphoria.

AMANDA AND THE GRAPE GAULTIER

Amanda Fox cared more about fashion than finances. Instead of returning the frantic calls of her accountant, she had spent the past two months glued to the insider blogs, obsessing over the perfect dress to wear to the fall season's biggest fashion benefit.

Finally, she found it. A Gaultier the color of Concord grapes, so sumptuous she knew every eye would be upon her at the event. The hem would skim her knee, revealing her spin class—sculpted calves. The neckline would drape as far as propriety allowed, and then imagination would take over.

She finally had the dress in hand, and it was even more beautiful than in the photographs.

"It's just the thing for this season," she murmured. "I'll take it, size two!"

It was so perfect that she did not even need to try it on. She handed over her sparkling Platinum Card and admired the sheen of the silk pooling on the counter. Her lips curled upward: no one at the gala would look more elegant than she would in this perfect purple dress.

The smiling shopgirl ran the card through the machine, and blinked her mile-long lashes. "Oh, dear," she said sweetly. "Mrs. Fox, you have been declined. Shall we try again or would you like to use another card?"

"Try again," said Amanda, scratching her wallet with her forefinger.

Declined. The shopgirl looked sorry, but she raised her sharp shears and snipped the shiny card in two nevertheless.

Amanda handed over her Gold Card. A line was forming behind her.

Snip.

She touched the purple silk and gave the salesgirl her Silver Card.

Snip. The salesgirl had stopped smiling. The line was getting longer. Amanda felt a strange heat in her stomach. She handed over her Pewter Card.

Snip.

"Another try, Mrs. Fox?"

"Oh, forget it," said Amanda, turning up her nose and heading for the door. "I'm sure I never would have worn it anyway. Purple is so last season."

IT IS EASY TO DESPISE
WHAT YOU CANNOT GET.

It was so **PERFECT** that she did not even need to try it on.

A
CATCALL
FOR
CARLA

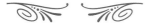

Carla was wearing a new dress, and she had just gotten her hair styled. As she walked along with her sister, she noticed a number of men whistling and waving.

"Fiona," she whispered. "You were right about this dress. Those guys can't stop staring."

"Carla," Fiona said. "Look behind you. There's a photo shoot in the park. They're looking at the model in the bikini."

THEY ARE NOT WISE WHO GIVE
TO THEMSELVES THE CREDIT DUE TO OTHERS.

CARPE
DIOR

Tracy was at the most talked about sample sale in the city. She had taken the morning off from work, traveled all the way downtown, and stood outside in the rain for three hours just to get in. She flipped through the dresses on the hangers and sighed. Boring, boring, boring, she thought.

At the other end of the aisle, Olivia was pushing her way through the dense racks. She had missed a prepaid session with a personal trainer in order to make it here, then stood in the rain and practically ruined her suede jacket, all in the name of finding something incredible to wear. Boring, she thought, flipping through the garments. Ugly! Boring, boring, boring.

Suddenly, there it was. That bag! *The* bag! *The* one! She had to have it—but there was Olivia, simultaneously grabbing the other strap. Tracy pulled, but Olivia wouldn't let her have it. It was her bag! She had wanted it all last spring! That buttery leather. That elegant shape! She hung on for all she was worth.

There they were: the great hunters, fighting over the spoils.

The two held on tight, and glared at each other.

"Oh no, you don't," said Tracy.

"Oh yes, I do," said Olivia.

A woman working at the sample sale saw them breathing heavily, flushed, in a disarray.

"You are absolutely *destroying* that gorgeous Dior," she said, snatching the purse and replacing it on the shelf. "When you finish arguing about who gets it, it will be right here."

"I saw it first," said Tracy.

"I touched it first," said Olivia.

While they argued, Samantha, who had just wandered into the sale, slipped around them.

"Pardon me," she said and walked toward the register, Dior in hand.

"Oh no, she didn't!" cried Olivia.

"Oh yes," said Tracy. "I believe she did."

IT SOMETIMES HAPPENS
THAT SOME WOMEN MAKE ALL
THE EFFORT, AND OTHERS
ALL THE PROFIT.

There they were: the great hunters,

fighting over the spoils.

EASY,
TWEEZY,
BEAUTIFUL

Bettina's eyes were looking beady. When she mentioned tweezing her brows to correct the problem to her older sister, Caroline rolled her own slightly beady eyes and told Bettina to leave well enough alone.

"Do what you want—but mine have never been the same again, I swear," said Caroline, an over-plucking survivor herself, who knew firsthand how difficult it was to grow one's eyebrows back.

Despite Caroline's advice, Bettina made an immediate appointment with her stylist, Javier, who twirled his tweezers and with a quick pinch, pinch, pinch made her look like a wide-eyed innocent.

"How's this for total ingénue?" he said, whipping her around to face the mirror.

She fluttered her lashes and was pleased.

That evening, she scrutinized her eyebrows in the mirror. Javier had missed a few hairs! She found her pink tweezers and plucked the left brow carefully. Pinch, pinch, pinch. Then the right. Pinch. Then she evened out the left one a little more. Now the right brow seemed to have an unusual slant—how annoying!

It didn't take long to even out her brows to nothing, save for an odd spare straggle. The space between her eyelids and her hairline was huge and vacant, an empty lot where a landmark used to be.

Moving quickly through horror, sadness, anger, and ultimately, depression, she drank three glasses of Chardonnay and went to sleep, hoping that when she woke up in the morning, her eyebrows would be back.

The next day, her dog kept barking at her. Her kids insisted they could walk to the bus stop—alone. Her husband suggested that they catch a Saturday-night movie—on cable. The barista at the coffee shop snickered when she ordered her skim-milk mochaccino.

Something had to be done.

A few days later, when her book club met at her house, Bettina showed off her new ultra-barefaced look, explaining to each of her friends how they too could benefit by a simple reduction of the brows. She told one that it would make her look younger, another that it would make her slimmer, and yet another that it would make her look smarter. Emma, always a follower, was about to submit to an overhaul, when Caroline spoke up.

"Oh, Bette," she said. "Sit down and be quiet. If you didn't look like a hairless cat you wouldn't be telling everyone else to whip out the wax."

MISERY LOVES COMPANY.

It didn't take long to even out her brows to nothing,

save for an odd, spare s t r a g g l e.

A GIRL
WITH CURLS

Chloë was a girl with golden curls. She had luscious locks, with tendrils that ran down her back like a river, yet she hated her hair. She coveted the sleeker styles of those lucky straight-haired women, who could wear chin-length bobs, who could let their hair down in the wind without worrying about knots and tangles, who didn't have high blood pressure because of fears about impending impenetrable frizziness when the weatherman talked about humidity.

Oh, how she longed to be one of the frizz-less flock!

She spent a month's rent to sit in a chair for three hours while two women pulled at her hair and rubbed chemicals that smelled like rotten eggs on her reddened scalp. This process made her hair feel like barbed wire, so she went to a salon where they used extracts from Peruvian sheep to keep the curl out and the moisture in. For three weeks she woke up with a greasy, stained pillowcase that smelled like a barn. Nonetheless, the curls returned too soon.

She gave up three vacations in two years, exchanging beach chairs and frosty margaritas in Anguilla, the gardens of Versailles, and a luxurious long weekend on Italy's Lake Como, where she *might* have had the chance to meet George Clooney, for Brazilian and Japanese and Egyptian treatments that offered the hope of turning her tangles into corn silk, just like her genetically blessed neighbors'.

One day at a new salon, while torturing her hair once again, she opened the latest *Vogue*. And there—in Beauty Trends—she encountered glossy images of models with curls that sprang forth: corkscrew ringlets; enormous Afros; long hair, uncombed and unparted and untended—masses of gorgeous, glorious waves.

She closed the magazine for a moment and checked the cover: yes, she *was* looking at *this month's issue*. Curls. Were. Back.

She leapt out of her chair and reached up with anxious fingers. But it was too late. The curls were gone, replaced at last by a silken swish that passed through her fingers like air. As she was leaving, she couldn't help but notice a bevy of straight-haired girls, who, having heard the decree that curly hair was all the rage, had alit for their scheduled perms.

THE DESIRE FOR IMAGINARY BENEFITS OFTEN INVOLVES THE LOSS OF PRESENT BLESSINGS.

OH, how she *longed* to be ONE of the *frizzless flock!*

LIKE
MOTHER,
LIKE
DAUGHTER

A mother picking up her daughter from school looked around at all of the girl's posh classmates and sighed.

"Gwendolyn Elizabeth Mary Catherine," she said. "What ever will become of you? Where is your grace, your style? Your hair is a mess. You insist on flapping about in those awful flip-flops. You look nothing like these other girls! I wish, for your sake, that you could be more elegant."

"Right," Gwendolyn said to her mother, who was fishing around for her car keys in the pants pocket of her worn-out, size-too-small, lilac velour tracksuit. "Show me the way, and I'll be right behind you."

EXAMPLE IS THE BEST PRECEPT.

Show me the way,

and I'll be right behind you.

BELLA

AND THE

MOUSE

Bella Brava, the ferociously brilliant and beautiful editor of *Moi* magazine, the world's most famous fashion publication, walked into her office to find Mimi, perhaps the meekest assistant she'd ever had, cowering over this month's proofs. The tiny girl had spilled Bella's double latte all over the pages and was trying to mop them up with her sleeve.

Bella pulled at her thick blond mane and looked around for something to throw at her. "All you had to do was bring the coffee!" she roared, her voice still hoarse from screaming at the features editor, Lillibeth. "Not redecorate my desk with it! You're fired! Collect your things and go!"

"Bella," Mimi began, the coffee cup shaking in her hand. "Ms. Brava! Please forgive me! Give me another chance and someday, I will repay you."

Bella laughed until she collapsed into her chair, then waved Mimi out of her office, saying, "Start by changing that awful shirt, you little mouse! And get me another latte! A double!"

Several months later, on the afternoon of *Moi*'s annual gala, Mimi was in the kitchen making Bella a fresh latte when she overheard Lillibeth whispering to Kate, another editor, just outside the doorway. That evening at the event, surrounded by fashionistas, Hollywood stars, and socialites, Bella would unveil a fabulous gown from the designer of the moment. The dress would be delivered to the office the day of the party, inspected by Bella herself, then sent up to her house in a limousine. With Kate's help, Lillibeth planned to intercept the dress en route to the car, unstitch an integral seam or two, and watch gleefully later when Bella's dress—and composure—unraveled in front of the world.

Once the editors were gone, Mimi went straight to Bella's office and told her of the plan to ruin her dress, giving her time to secure a second gown even better than the first and have it sent directly home.

"See?" said Mimi. "I told you I would be able to help you."

Bella smiled at the tiny girl and said, "Don't push it."

LITTLE FRIENDS MAY PROVE
GREAT FRIENDS.

INTELLIGENT DESIGN

A designer had a vision of the most divine jacket—crunchy wool bouclé cleverly cut into the perfect elongated silhouette with a coy collar—upon which he could hinge his entire autumn collection. He grabbed his sketch pad and began to draw.

As he penciled in the outlines of the coat, he imagined the impact of his design. "Once the public sees what I have done, my name will be on everybody's lips. The coat will mark the beginning of my rightful place in haute couture. And once I establish *ma grande maison de la couture en Paris*, with appointment-only boutiques in Milan, Rome, London, and New York, that will feed the market for my ready-to-wear lines in every conceivable city *dans le monde!*"

As he sketched in a figure, he considered what the expansion of his brand could lead to—menswear, sportswear, wedding, a baby line—even pets!

The possibilities were *infini*! As he shaded in the jacket, he thought, "These diffusion lines—*bien sûr*—will feed my exceptional accessory and fragrance lines—not to mention home and garden furnishings!"

As he initialed the drawing, he realized, "I will be the biggest designer in the world! Bigger than Karl Lagerfeld or Marc Jacobs! I will be the Dior of this century! *Et voilà!*"

He stood up and went to show his magnificent design to his assistant.

"I have that jacket," she said. "I got it last week at the shop down the block."

And with that, his glamorous empire crumbled in an instant.

DON'T COUNT YOUR CHICKENS
UNTIL THEY ARE HATCHED.

"I will be **the biggest DESIGNER** *in the world!*

Bigger than Karl Lagerfeld or Marc Jacobs!

I will be the *Dior* OF THIS CENTURY!"

THE RED CHOOS

Honey had been four foot ten since she was twelve. As nature had not given her the extra few inches she needed, she found them herself. By the time she turned fourteen, she had achieved a nearly Zen-like focus when it came to her ability to teeter around on four-inch stilettos 24/7 without giving a thought to the pain. By the time she was twenty-three, four-inch heels were child's play. She had mastered her stride in five-, even six-inch heels. So what if her feet complained?

If a shoe did not have an extremely high heel, it was not a shoe. When ballet flats became fashionable again, she scoffed. When her friends wore sneakers, she sneered. Honey kept herself a step above them, literally. Flats were for little girls. And sneakers? Sneakers were for little boys.

There were no exceptions. She wore heels to take out the trash. She had a rubber pair with traction for snow days. She had a clear plastic pair made for the beach. She even had a pair of rubber-soled heels for the gym!

One Monday morning, while her colleagues soft-shoed their way through the city streets and changed into work-appropriate pumps at their desks, Honey stepped into her red snakeskin Jimmy Choos, clicked her way out of her apartment, down the usual designated streets and avenues, and into the marbled lobby of her office building. She rode the elevator up twenty-five flights, judging all the women around her and their awful choices in footwear as usual: running shoes, Crocs, Uggs, ballet flats, work boots—even a pair of flip-flops!

At noon, the emergency bell went off. The floor fire chief called them all to the stairwell. "This is a practice," she said. "Not an actual emergency. But we have to walk down."

Honey watched as all her sensibly soled coworkers took to the stairs. In her Choos, she tried to follow, but she couldn't keep up.

"Honey," said the fire chief. "Take off your shoes. We have to hurry."

Honey took off her Choos, but oddly enough, was unable to release her heels. Thus held back, she had to be carried down by two mailroom boys, to the great amusement of everybody but poor Honey, whose feet were stuck permanently in tiptoe.

PLEASURE BOUGHT WITH PAINS, HURTS.

If a shoe did not have an extremely high heel,

it was not a shoe.

ODE TO JOY

Arabella Perkins wanted to be happy, so she bought a great, big, beautiful bottle of Joy. Every day, she would sit and look through the glass, imagining the fragrance of the world's costliest, most delicate, most renowned perfume. But she couldn't bring herself to open the bottle, afraid that even releasing the stopper would lessen the value of the scent, sure that each drop worn would be a drop lost, a drop of Joy she would never have again.

"Look," she said to her daughter, Ruby, when she was only ten years old. "They say it is made from a million roses."

"May I try some?" asked the girl.

"No," said her mother. "I'm saving it for a special occasion."

"Look," she said to her neighbor Julia Clover, the mother of Ruby's best friend, Daniel. "They say it smells better than the rarest lily."

"May I try some?" asked Julia.

"No," said Arabella. "I'm saving it."

Many, many years later, on the day Ruby was to marry Daniel, she asked her mother if she could wear some Joy. Arabella, almost roused to sentiment by the occasion, said no. "I am happy today," she thought to herself. "But I should save the Joy for another day." And some years after that, when Julia asked her if she could borrow some Joy to wear to Daniel's graduation from medical school, Arabella marveled at her son-in-law's success and offered her congratulations, but she would not share the Joy.

"No," she said. "I'm saving it." Julia is happy, she thought to herself. Why does she need more Joy?

～

"Look," she said to the cat, when everybody else had stopped calling. "Joy! They say it smells like the wind after it rains."

"*Meow*," said her fat tabby.

One day, while Arabella was out running errands, the cat walked across her dresser and knocked the bottle of Joy on its side, loosening the stopper so that all the liquid spilled on the floor and evaporated. By the time she came home, the Joy was gone; not even a lingering trace remained.

Upon discovering the mishap, she ran to Julia's door, weeping about her loss.

"You'll survive," said Julia, rolling her eyes. "Just refill the bottle with water and close the stopper. What's the difference? You have no idea what real Joy is."

TRUE VALUE IS NOT IN POSSESSION BUT IN USE.

HERMES BALMAIN
PRADA
DIOR GIVENCHY
Scar de la Renta
FENDI GUCCI

LOUIS VU
VAL

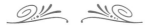

BEST
DRESSED

A woman who was well traveled often bragged about her journeys. In particular, she was in the habit of going on about her exquisite acquisitions, carefully detailing the gorgeous dresses, sumptuous scarves and wraps, divine footwear, and one-of-a-kind jewelry she had discovered in the most fashionable cities across the world. In Milan, she said, she found the most chic vintage evening gowns, and in Hong Kong, silks to rival the most vividly colored blooms. In Barcelona, she had found rich velvets and in London, corsets that could cinch a round woman to an hourglass.

One of her neighbors interrupted her, finally.

"My dear," she said. "If your taste is really so magnificent, wearing the clothes should be enough."

SHE WHO DOES A THING WELL
HAS NO NEED TO BOAST.

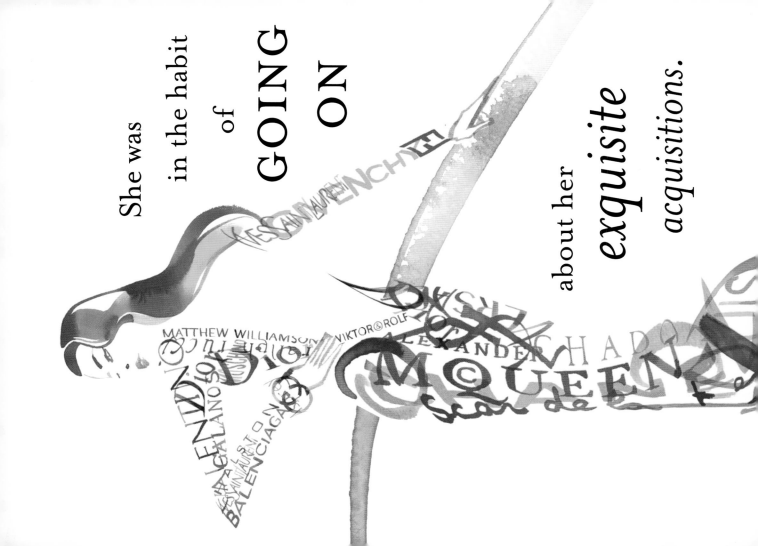

She was in the habit of GOING ON about her *exquisite* acquisitions.

BIRDS
OF A
FEATHER

Whether for her chart-busting music or her outrageous ensembles, Lady La-Di-Dah always made headlines. Whatever she wore broke some kind of rule, then rewrote it. Feathers, chains, leather, plastic wrap, even scraps of grade-A sirloin: there was no substance she would not don if it were possible to affix it securely to her perfectly toned body. She was a rare bird with a style all her own, and Lucy adored her.

Lucy was watching the music awards when Lady La-Di-Dah stepped onto the red carpet in a gown of pink feathers with a crown to match, long, pink-feathered gloves, and a live peacock on a chain. The peacock was too much, but the gown! The gown was spectacular! Lucy watched as the crowd and paparazzi went wild, applauding and screaming her name as she made her way into the auditorium.

A few days later, Lucy's lawyer, Nicholas, who had always had a thing for her, invited her to a gallery opening downtown. She accepted, and then rifled through her closet. She had a row of new dresses, but after seeing Lady's incredible getup, they just all looked so *normal*. What she needed was some flair—a newer, more vibrant style. And so inspired, Lucy decided to craft her own.

With a big bag of pink feathers, a glue gun, some rhinestones, and some sequins, Lucy took her plainest dress and a tiara she had bought at the local party shop and went to town. She covered them top to bottom in layers of feathers, then added sequins and rhinestones, scattering a few through the feathers like little stars in a pink sky. She would be the star of the show!

At the opening, though, Nicholas started chuckling as soon as he saw her, then quickly deposited her in a corner with a glass of pinot grigio. No one spoke to her the entire night, which was, she thought, odd, as they were all staring at her.

Finally, after an hour or two of drinking solo, Lucy wobbled out to the street in her now-molting dress to hail a taxi.

In her wake, all she heard was laughter.

IT IS ABSURD TO MIMIC OTHERS.

She would be the star of the show!

GRACIOUS LIVING

Addison thought that Paige was very beautiful and elegant, and she wanted to be as graceful and gracious as she perceived her friend to be.

She knew that Paige wore only the finest cashmere sweaters from Scotland, so she bought a row full of sweaters just like hers.

She heard that Paige worked out with a famous celebrity trainer, so she took on extra hours at work so she could afford to work out with starlets and socialites, too.

When Paige mentioned reading poetry, Addison went out and bought an anthology.

When Paige told her that she would be vacationing in Saint Bart's, Addison bought a ticket and reserved a room at the same boutique hotel.

When Paige got blond highlights, Addison got some, too.

Really, Addison thought, she must be just like Paige, now.

The two were out together one afternoon, when they walked by a young man sitting on the sidewalk with a sign that said, "Hungry. Please help."

Addison didn't even notice. She was too busy thinking about how gracious she was.

Paige slowed her pace, smiled at the man, then slipped ten dollars into his cup, thinking of how fortunate she was to live such a privileged life.

CHANGE OF HABIT CANNOT ALTER NATURE.

SHE wanted TO BE as *graceful* and *gracious*

as she *perceived* her *friend* TO BE.

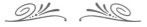

MODEL
BEHAVIOR

"**H**elp!!!" cried the young model in the pale lemon chiffon. "This gown is too tight! I can't breathe!"

A team of seamstresses rushed to fit her properly before they sent her down the runway, and she laughed merrily at their distress.

"Just kidding!" said Annika. "It isn't too tight! It's perfect."

Next day, next designer, next dress: the same young model sounded the alarm backstage.

"Help!" cried Annika, pulling at the ruched yak skin around her tiny waist. "The gown is too tight! I can't breathe!"

The seamstresses rushed again to her aid, and she laughed, reassuring them that the dress fit perfectly and the show would go smoothly.

Show after show, Annika would repeat her little joke, and then giggle.

On the night before the last day of Fashion Week, she went out with a bunch of the girls to celebrate. Without exactly meaning to, she ate a bowlful of gnocchi, a half loaf of bread, and a plateful of tiramisu. After all, she had been living on plain lettuce for more than two weeks!

The next day, at the final show, she slipped into her first dress—and it was much too tight.

"Help!" Annika called, frantic, tugging at the zipper. She was next in line and this just would not do. She cursed the pasta and gasped for assistance. "Help! This dress is too tight! I—can't—breathe!"

But the seamstresses ignored her, knowing her little joke all too well by this time, and continued helping the other girls. With no alternative, Annika staggered breathlessly down the runway with her dress half-zipped to the waist, much to the amused bewilderment of the crowd, the fury of the designer, and the embarrassment of her agency.

She was banned immediately from modeling and, in disgrace, returned to her post as cashier at the little tourist shop specializing in Little Mermaid memorabilia in Copenhagen Harbor, where she had been discovered just a few months before.

THERE IS NO BELIEVING A LIAR,
EVEN WHEN SHE SPEAKS THE TRUTH.

NEXT *day,*

NEXT *designer,*

NEXT *dress...*

A BIRKIN
IN THE
HAND

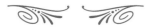

Camille and Marie were chatting over a cappuc-
cino at the department-store café.

"How did you do?" asked Camille. "I found
a lime green patent clutch, a cream suede clutch,
a brown ostrich hobo, a striped lizard safari bag, a
salmon croc tote, a black bucket zebra and calfskin bag,
and a navy blue python shoulder bag. All on sale!"

"Still just the one," said Marie, holding up her
beige bag.

"Oh, Marie," said Camille. "I wish you could
spoil yourself a little! Look at me, I have all of these
beautiful handbags for the season, a new one for every
day! Are you sure you don't want a new purse?"

"Quite sure," said Marie, smiling gently. "True,
I only have one. But that one is a custom-made
Birkin."

QUALITY IS BETTER THAN QUANTITY.

THE Original AESOP'S Fables

THE ANT AND THE GRASSHOPPER

In a field one summer's day a Grasshopper was hopping about, chirping and singing to its heart's content. An Ant passed by, bearing along with great toil an ear of corn he was taking to the nest. "Why not come and chat with me," said the Grasshopper, "instead of toiling and moiling in that way?" "I am helping to lay up food for the winter," said the Ant, "and recommend you to do the same." "Why bother about winter?" said the Grasshopper; we have got plenty of food at present." But the Ant went on its way and continued its toil. When the winter came the Grasshopper had no food and found itself dying of hunger, while it saw the ants distributing every day corn and grain from the stores they had collected in the summer. Then the Grasshopper knew:

It is best to prepare for the days of necessity.

THE ASS AND HIS MASTERS

An Ass, belonging to an herb-seller who gave him too little food and too much work made a petition to Jupiter to be released from his present service and provided with another master. Jupiter, after warning him that he would repent his request, caused him to be sold to a tile-maker. Shortly afterwards, finding that he had heavier loads to carry and harder work in the brick-field, he petitioned for another change of master. Jupiter, telling him that it would be the last time that he could grant his request, ordained that he be sold to a tanner. The Ass found that he had fallen into worse hands, and noting his master's occupation, said, groaning: "It would have been better for me to have been either starved by the one, or to have been overworked by the other of my former masters, than to have been bought by my present owner, who will even after I am dead tan my hide, and make me useful to him."

He that finds discontentment in one place is not likely to find happiness in another.

THE FOX AND THE GRAPES

One hot summer's day a Fox was strolling through an orchard till he came to a bunch of Grapes just ripening on a vine which had been trained over a lofty branch. "Just the thing to quench my thirst," said he. Drawing back a few paces, he took a run and a jump, and just missed the bunch. Turning round again with a One, Two, Three, he jumped up, but with no greater success. Again and again he tried after the tempting morsel, but at last had to give it up, and walked away with his nose in the air, saying: "I am sure they are sour."

It is easy to despise what you cannot get.

THE ASS CARRYING THE IMAGE

An Ass once carried through the streets of a city a famous wooden Image, to be placed in one of its Temples. As he passed along, the crowd made lowly prostration before the Image. The Ass, thinking that they bowed their heads in token of respect for himself, bristled up with pride, gave himself airs, and refused to move another step. The driver, seeing him thus stop, laid his whip lustily about his shoulders and said, "O you perverse dull-head! It is not yet come to this, that men pay worship to an Ass."

They are not wise who give to themselves the credit due to others.

THE LION, THE BEAR, AND THE FOX

A Lion and a Bear seized a Kid at the same moment, and fought fiercely for its possession. When they had fearfully lacerated each other and were faint from the long combat, they lay down exhausted with fatigue. A Fox, who had gone around them at a distance several times, saw them both stretched on the ground with the Kid lying untouched in the middle. He ran in between them, and seizing the Kid, scampered off as fast as he could. The Lion and the Bear saw him, but not being able to get up, said, "Woe be to us, that we should have fought and belabored ourselves only to serve the turn of a Fox."

It sometimes happens that one man has all the toil, and another all the profit.

THE FOX WHO HAD LOST HIS TAIL

A Fox caught in a trap escaped, but in so doing lost his tail. Thereafter, feeling his life a burden from the shame and ridicule to which he was exposed, he schemed to convince all the other Foxes that being tailless was much more attractive, thus making up for his own deprivation. He assembled a good many Foxes and publicly advised them to cut off their tails, saying that they would not only look much better without them, but that they would get rid of the weight of the brush, which was a very great inconvenience. One of them interrupting him said, "If you had not yourself lost your tail, my friend, you would not thus counsel us."

Misery loves company.

THE KITES AND THE SWANS

The Kites of olden times, as well as the Swans, had the privilege of song. But having heard the neigh of the horse, they were so enchanted with the sound, that they tried to imitate it; and, in trying to neigh, they forgot how to sing.

The desire for imaginary benefits often involves the loss of present blessings.

THE TWO CRABS

One fine day two Crabs came out from their home to take a stroll on the sand. "Child," said the mother, "you are walking very ungracefully. You should accustom yourself, to walking straight forward without twisting from side to side." "Pray, mother," said the young one, "do but set the example yourself, and I will follow you."

Example is the best precept.

THE LION AND THE MOUSE

Once when a Lion was asleep a little Mouse began running up and down upon him; this soon wakened the Lion, who placed his huge paw upon him, and opened his big jaws to swallow him. "Pardon, O King," cried the little Mouse: "forgive me this time, I shall never forget it: who knows but what I may be able to do you a turn some of these days?" The Lion was so tickled at the idea of the Mouse being able to help him, that he lifted up his paw and let him go. Some time after, the Lion was caught in a trap, and the hunters who desired to carry him alive to the King, tied him to a tree while they went in search of a wagon to carry him on. Just then the little Mouse happened to pass by, and seeing the Lion's sad plight, went up to him and soon gnawed away the ropes that bound the King of the Beasts. "Was I not right?" said the little Mouse.

Little friends may prove great friends.

THE MILK WOMAN AND HER PAIL

A farmer's daughter was carrying her pail of milk from the field to the farmhouse, when she fell a-musing. "The money for which this milk will be sold, will buy at least three hundred eggs. The eggs, allowing for all mishaps, will produce two hundred and fifty chickens. The chickens will become ready for the market when poultry will fetch the highest price, so that by the end of the year I shall have money enough from my share to buy a new gown. In this dress I will go to the Christmas parties, where all the young fellows will propose to me, but I will toss my head and refuse them every one." At this moment she tossed her head in unison with her thoughts, when down fell the milk pail to the ground, and all her imaginary schemes perished in a moment.

Don't count your chickens before they are hatched.

THE FLIES AND THE HONEY-POT

A number of Flies were attracted to a jar of honey which had been overturned in a house-keeper's room, and placing their feet in it, ate greedily. Their feet, however, became so smeared with the honey that they could not use their wings, nor release themselves, and were suffocated. Just as they were expiring, they exclaimed, "O foolish creatures that we are, for the sake of a little pleasure we have destroyed ourselves."

Pleasure bought with pains, hurts.

THE MISER

A Miser sold all that he had and bought a lump of gold, which he buried in a hole in the ground by the side of an old wall and went to look at daily. One of his workmen observed his frequent visits to the spot and decided to watch his movements. He soon discovered the secret of the hidden treasure, and digging down, came to the lump of gold, and stole it. The Miser, on his next visit, found the hole empty and began to tear his hair and to make loud lamentations. A neighbor, seeing him overcome with grief and learning the cause, said, "Pray do not grieve so; but go and take a stone, and place it in the hole, and fancy that the gold is still lying there. It will do you quite the same service; for when the gold was there, you had it not, as you did not make the slightest use of it."

The true value of money is not in its possession but in its use.

THE BOASTING TRAVELER

A man who had traveled in foreign lands boasted very much, on returning to his own country, of the many wonderful and heroic feats he had performed in the different places he had visited. Among other things, he said that when he was at Rhodes he had leaped to such a distance that no man of his day could leap anywhere near him as to that, there were in Rhodes many persons who saw him do it and whom he could call as witnesses. One of the bystanders interrupted him, saying: "Now, my good man, if this be all true there is no need of witnesses. Suppose this to be Rhodes, and leap for us."

He who does a thing well does not need to boast.

THE MONKEY AND THE CAMEL

The beasts of the forest gave a splendid entertainment at which the Monkey stood up and danced. Having vastly delighted the assembly, he sat down amidst universal applause. The Camel, envious of the praises bestowed on the Monkey and desiring to divert to himself the favor of the guests, proposed to stand up in his turn and dance for their amusement. He moved about in so utterly ridiculous a manner that the Beasts, in a fit of indignation, set upon him with clubs and drove him out of the assembly.

It is absurd to ape our betters.

THE RAVEN AND THE SWAN

A Raven saw a Swan and desired to secure for himself the same beautiful plumage. Supposing that the Swan's splendid white color arose from his washing in the water in which he swam, the Raven left the altars in the neighborhood where he picked up his living, and took up residence in the lakes and pools. But cleansing his feathers as often as he would, he could not change their color, while through want of food he perished.

Change of habit cannot alter Nature.

THE SHEPHERD'S BOY AND THE WOLF

A Shepherd Boy who watched a flock of sheep near a village, brought out the villagers three or four times by crying out, "Wolf! Wolf!" and when his neighbors came to help him, laughed at them for their pains. The Wolf, however, did truly come at last. The Shepherd Boy, now really alarmed, shouted in an agony of terror: "Pray, do come and help me; the Wolf is killing the sheep"; but no one paid any heed to his cries, nor rendered any assistance. The Wolf, having no cause of fear, at his leisure lacerated or destroyed the whole flock.

There is no believing a liar, even when he speaks the truth.

THE VIXEN AND THE LIONESS

A Vixen who was taking her babies out for an airing one balmy morning, came across a Lioness, with her cub in arms. "Why such airs, haughty dame, over one solitary cub?" sneered the Vixen. "Look at my healthy and numerous litter here, and imagine, if you are able, how a proud mother should feel." The Lioness gave her a squelching look, and lifting up her nose, walked away, saying calmly, "Yes, just look at that beautiful collection. What are they? Foxes! I've only one, but remember, that one is a Lion."

Quality is better than quantity.

ABOUT THE AUTHOR

Sandra Bark is a *New York Times* bestselling author who collaborates on books with notable figures. Her projects include the bestsellers *The Tattoo Chronicles* and *High Voltage Tattoo* by Kat Von D, *You Know You Want It*, the style manual by Eric Daman, Emmy Award–winning costume designer for *Gossip Girl*, and *Tracy Anderson's 30-Day Method* by celebrity trainer Tracy Anderson. The founder and curator of the street art blog the Scenic Sidewalk, www.thescenicsidewalk.com, Sandra lives and works in Brooklyn, New York.

ABOUT THE ILLUSTRATOR

Bil Donovan is a fashion illustrator whose work has appeared in various publications and advertising campaigns worldwide. His numerous clients include Neiman Marcus, Estée Lauder, Givenchy, ESCADA, Yves Saint Laurent, and Mercedes-Benz. A brand ambassador for Christian Dior Beauty, he teaches fashion illustration at the Fashion Institute of Technology. He is the author of *Advanced Fashion Drawing: Lifestyle Illustration* and the illustrator of *The Dress Doctor*. He lives in New York City.